AVA and the RAINBOW

(WHO STAYED)

Ged Adamson

AVA and the RAINBOW
(WHO STAYED)

Ged Adamson

HARPER
An Imprint of HarperCollins Publishers

For Chuca

Ava and the Rainbow (Who Stayed)
Copyright © 2018 by Ged Adamson
All rights reserved. Manufactured in China.
No part of this book may be used or reproduced in any manner whatsoever without written permission
except in the case of brief quotations embodied in critical articles and reviews. For information address
HarperCollins Children's Books, a division of HarperCollins Publishers, 195 Broadway, New York, NY 10007.

www.harpercollinschildrens.com

ISBN 978-0-06-267080-9

The artist used pencil, watercolor and Photoshop to create the digital illustrations for this book.
Design by Ged Adamson and Chelsea C. Donaldson
17 18 19 20 21   SCP   10 9 8 7 6 5 4 3 2 1

❖
First Edition

AVA was excited. Not because the rain was stopping.

She was excited because the sun was coming out. And that meant one thing.

A rainbow!

And this really was the most beautiful rainbow Ava had ever seen.

"If only you could stay forever," she said.

That night, Ava dreamed the
rainbow did stay forever.

yawn!

"What a happy dream," she thought as she woke the next morning.

But when she looked out her window, Ava wondered if she had actually woken up at all.

The rainbow was still there!

And when he was still there that night,
Ava realized it was true.

The rainbow really *had* decided to stay!

Within days, people were arriving from far and wide.

Everybody wanted to see the rainbow who had decided to stay.

The town was quick to make the most of it.

There was a new town mascot.

Which didn't please the old town mascot.

The shops were suddenly full of rainbow-themed souvenirs.

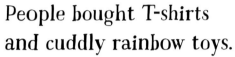

People bought T-shirts and cuddly rainbow toys.

And the rainbow was discussed by the professors in the town university.

Every week something different was happening.

And the rainbow was at the center of it all.

Ava would spend hours talking to the
rainbow. She told him all about herself.

She introduced him to her friends.

She sang to him.

And she showed him all her favorite books and toys.

Winter came, and it was the coldest anyone could remember.

The **rainbow** shivered and shook, but still, he stayed.

Spring finally arrived, and by this time
people had gotten so used to the rainbow,
sometimes they even forgot he was there.

Ava began to realize something.

Slowly but surely . . .

. . . the town was losing interest in the rainbow.

The rainbow was no longer
at the center of it all.

"How could they do this to something so special?" Ava said in despair.

Just then, a crowd of people with cameras came into view, climbing the hill toward them.

"I think they're all coming to see you again!" shouted Ava to the rainbow.

But it wasn't the rainbow they'd come to see.
Perched on a tree was a tiny bird.

"Isn't it wonderful?" said one of the people
breathlessly. "It's a Russian water sparrow!
We're so lucky! They stop here for only a few
hours every year. Such a rare and precious sight!"

Ava didn't know it, but the rainbow had heard every word.

"Hmm," he thought, "*a rare and precious sight.*"

And the next morning the rainbow was gone.

Ava hoped he wouldn't be gone forever.

From that moment on, every time it rained,
Ava looked for the rainbow.

And then one special day the rainbow
had returned!

Ava knew this time the rainbow
wouldn't stay forever, but he'd
always come back . . .

a rare and precious sight indeed.